CW00855035

FOLENS
IDEAS BANK
BRITAIN SINCE 1930

Neil Tonge
Peter Hepplewhite

Contents

Folens
Publishers

How to use this book

Ideas Bank books provide ready to use, practical, photocopiable activity pages for children, **plus** a wealth of ideas for extension and development.

TEACHER IDEAS PAGE   PHOTOCOPIABLE ACTIVITY PAGE

Clear focus to the activity.

Key questions.

Historical background information.

Suggestions for developing work on the photocopiable pages.

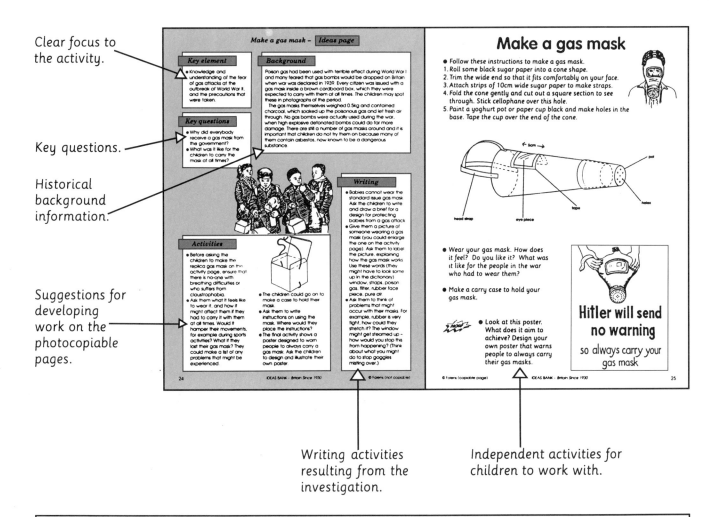

Writing activities resulting from the investigation.

Independent activities for children to work with.

Folens allows photocopying of pages marked 'copiable page' for educational use, providing that this use is within the confines of the purchasing institution. Copiable pages should not be declared in any return in respect of any photocopying licence.

Folens books are protected by international copyright laws. All rights are reserved. The copyright of all materials in this book, except where otherwise stated, remains the property of the publisher and authors. No part of this publication may be reproduced, stored in a retrieval system, or transmitted, in any form or by any means, for whatever purpose, without the written permission of Folens Limited.

This resource may be used in a variety of ways. However, it is not intended that teachers or children should write directly into the book itself.

Neil Tonge and Peter Hepplewhite hereby assert their moral rights to be identified as the authors of this work in accordance with the Copyright, Designs and Patents Act 1988.

Editor: Claire Ancell   Layout artist: Suzanne Ward

Illustrations: Jane Bottomley   Cover image: Hulton Deutsch   Cover design: In Touch Creative Services

© 1996 Folens Limited, on behalf of the author(s).

Folens would like to acknowledge Lancaster City Museums for the use of the illustration on p41.

Every effort has been made to contact copyright holders of material used in this book. If any have been overlooked, we will be pleased to make any necessary arrangements.

British Library Cataloguing in Publication Data. A catalogue record for this book is available from the British Library.

First published 1996 by Folens Limited, Dunstable and Dublin.

Folens Limited, Albert House, Apex Business Centre, Boscombe Road, Dunstable, LU5 4RL, England.

ISBN 1 85276755-3

Printed in Singapore by Craft Print.

Introduction

The period of history from the 1930s to the present day has seen an increasing amount of change. There have been enormous advances in technology and material comforts. However, not all have shared in the benefits, either in Britain or the world at large. It is also a period which has often seen the mass destruction caused by war.

The first activities are designed to highlight some of the major themes of the period. Overviews of key events are presented in 'Using newspapers' and 'From Empire to Commonwealth', with the latter describing the decline of Britain as a major power in the world. Social themes are picked up throughout the book. Topics include the roles of women, employment and the increasing use of the motor car.

Each age reinterprets previous ones. Our own is no exception. With the advent of television, certain images may have a powerful influence in forming opinions and attitudes. 'Memories of the 1930s' asks children to consider how images of the past are manipulated for both personal and public reasons.

Strong images of the 1930s survive. They are examined in a number of activities. 'The changes in housing' and 'Housing conditions' prompt children to consider the differences between their domestic lives and those of people in the 1930s. Other strong images of this period are those of unemployment and 'Living on the dole'. This activity attempts to bring home the reality of being unemployed, with emphasis on the financial difficulties of the average family. It also discusses the causes and effects of unemployment.

World War II was a harrowing time for the British people. Many schools focus heavily on this period, extending the unit by looking at features of the Home Front in their locality. It is therefore allocated a higher proportion of activities. The emphasis is on the social aspects of fighting a total war, explaining, among other things, mass bombing, rationing, evacuation, the threat of gas attacks, changes in employment patterns and propaganda.

For many, the Coronation of Queen Elizabeth represented the hopeful return to a golden age for the nation. Meanwhile, fundamental changes were under way which would alter the future image of Britain in another way entirely. The increase in prosperity among teenagers produced a succession of youth cultures which did not adhere to the values and expectations of previous generations of Britons. This theme is explored in 'Fashion in the Sixties'. Simultaneously, the notion of 'Britain' itself was undergoing significant change. The nation began to experience huge cultural differences under the influence of the American lifestyle, Commonwealth immigration and the European Economic Community. 'Changing food habits' looks at the changes that have occurred in Britain's eating customs because of these factors.

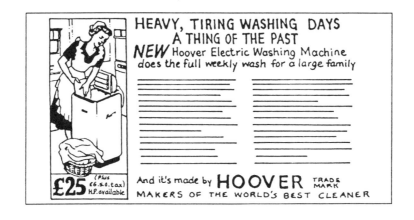

HEAVY, TIRING WASHING DAYS
A THING OF THE PAST
NEW Hoover Electric Washing Machine does the full weekly wash for a large family

£25 (Plus £6.50 tax) H.P. available

And it's made by HOOVER TRADE MARK
MAKERS OF THE WORLD'S BEST CLEANER

Using newspapers – Ideas page

Key element

- The chronology of Britain since 1930, using newspapers for historical enquiry.

Key questions

- What is a newspaper headline?
- How does it sum up events?

Activities

- Cut out the headlines on the activity page and glue them on to the timeline in chronological order.
- Discuss how a headline helps to sell a newspaper. Why must they be short and snappy? Look at the headlines in 'quality' and 'tabloid' newspapers for one day. Why is there a difference? Consider the audience that is being targeted and the style of the newspaper.
- Look back to the last history unit the children studied and make up ten headlines to cover the main events of the period. For example, 12 July 1588, 'Armada sets sail from Spain'.
- Discuss each of the headlines shown on the activity page. What are they about? Which is the most important headline, and why?
- Listen to a short radio news broadcast and make up headlines for the day.

Background

Newspaper headlines give us a quirky history of the twentieth century. They focus on tragedy, firsts and lasts, achievements, celebrities and human drama. The *Daily Express* banner for the *Sputnik* launch in 1957, 'SPACE AGE IS HERE', captured the event and its implications perfectly.

As well as national papers, most communities had a local press from the mid-eighteenth century. Excellent classroom material can be found for studies of local history and the Victorians as well as Britain since 1930. Advertisements can bring a period to life for younger children, with illustrations such as clothes, foods and modes of transport.

Other themes that can be explored include births, deaths and marriages; house sales; crime reports; disasters; trials; prices of goods and services; the opening or closure of factories and local or national planning controversies.

Local libraries often have comprehensive indexes of articles in local papers.

Thursday February 23 1933

CAMPBELL SHATTERS ALL RECORDS

Monday January 31 1972

BELFAST'S BLOODY SUNDAY

Writing

- Ask the children to make a table like this one. They could fill it in with headlines from the activity sheet, in chronological order.

Date	Decade	Headline
Friday August 15, 1969	1960s	Ulster Gun Battles

- Set a research task. Ask the children to make up their own headlines for a Headline History display for one decade. Events covered in the 1930s, for example, might include the Jarrow March, Malcolm Campbell's land speed record and the abdication of Edward VIII.

          © Folens (not copiable)

Headline history

Newspaper headlines can sum up history in a few words.

● Cut out the headlines and the timeline. Glue the timeline along the middle of a new sheet of paper. Arrange the headlines along it according to the decade in which they happened. Use the space above and below the timeline.

Monday July 21 1969

MAN WALKS ON MOON

September 4 1939

OUR FIRST DAY AT WAR: CHURCHILL IS NEW NAVY CHIEF

Wednesday June 15 1982

BRITAIN VICTORIOUS IN FALKLANDS

Tuesday August 7 1945

ATOMIC BOMB CHANGES THE WORLD
Japs hit hard by secret weapon

Monday January 31 1972

BELFAST'S BLOODY SUNDAY

Friday November 23 1990

THATCHER BETRAYED BY HER OWN CABINET

Saturday October 5 1957

SOVIET SATELLITE CIRCLES THE EARTH

| 1930s |
| 1940s |
| 1950s |
| 1960s |
| 1970s |
| 1980s |
| 1990s |

● Make up a headline for your birth and for the birth of one of your grandparents. Add these to the timeline.

From Empire to Commonwealth – Ideas page

Key elements

- Knowledge and understanding of the terms 'Empire' and 'Commonwealth', and the changes in Britain's role in the world since the 1930s.

Key questions

- How big was Britain's Empire?
- When and why did former colonies gain independence?
- What is the Commonwealth?

Background

The British Empire reached its peak in 1933, covering almost a quarter of the world's land surface and embracing a quarter of its population (about 500 million people). This created a false impression of great strength. In fact, British power depended on the country's economic and military resources, and these were in decline. During World War II, much of the Empire in Asia fell to the Japanese and had to be won back. After 1945, the British had neither the strength nor the will to attempt to hold parts of the Empire by force.

After World War II, many countries began to demand their freedom. By the end of the 1960s they had gained independence. However, most decided to keep their links with Britain, and each other, by joining the Commonwealth.

India took independence in 1947. This was followed by rapid decolonisation elsewhere, in the Middle East in the 1950s, and Africa and the West Indies in the 1960s. This was often done amicably, and the Commonwealth has come to represent one of the great friendly groups of nations in the world. Its membership currently stands at 51 countries.

Activities

- Use an atlas to connect Commonwealth countries to their names on the lists. Recent country names have been used.
- Ask the children to suggest why Britain decided to give up the Empire rather than fight to hold it. For example, the Empire was too big and too far away; Britain was weak after the war; countries had the right to self-rule; it had become very expensive to maintain.
- Prepare a Commonwealth display, with maps of member countries, their capital cities and flags.
- For cross-curricular links with geography, contrast your locality with a locality in a country such as Bangladesh, India or Canada. The Commonwealth Institute offers a variety of resources for sale or loan (telephone The Commonwealth Resource Centre at 0171 603 4535, extension 210).

Country	Life expectancy (1992)	Calories per person per day (1988)
Australia	77	3,302
Bangladesh	53	2,037
Botswana	68	2,260
Britain	76	3,270
Canada	78	3,242
India	60	2,229

- Find the remaining places ruled by Britain on a map or globe: The Falkland Islands, Ascension Island, Hong Kong (until 1997), British Antarctic territory and Gibraltar. Judging from their location, might any other countries be annoyed at Britain ruling them, for example China, Argentina or Spain?

Writing

- Ask the children to use a dictionary or a thesaurus to prepare word lists that explain what 'Empire' and 'independence' mean. Discuss why peoples and nations value independence so much.
- Use the word lists to prepare a written display in which each child contributes a sentence or two such as 'Empire means...being ruled by another country' or 'Independence means... choosing your own government.'

Independence means... choosing your own government

Empire means... being ruled by another country

Empire to Commonwealth

Here is a world map that shows Britain and the Empire in 1901.

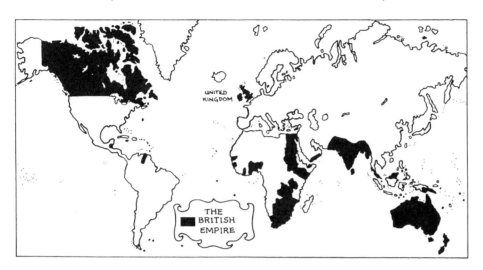

These maps show the countries of the Empire in Africa and Asia. The lists name these countries and the dates they became independent.
● Draw lines from the country name to its place on the map.

South Africa **1961**
Egypt **1956**
Somalia **1960**
Malawi **1964**
Zimbabwe **1980**
Yemen **1967**
Lesotho **1966**
Tanzania **1964**
Kenya **1963**

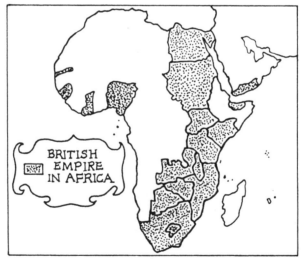

Ghana **1957**
Nigeria **1960**
Zambia **1964**
Gambia **1965**
Uganda **1960**
Sierra Leone **1961**
Sudan **1956**
Botswana **1966**

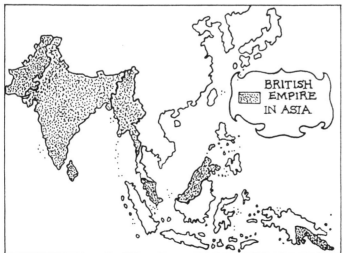

Pakistan **1947**
East Pakistan **1947**
(Bangladesh **1971**)
Burma **1948**
Papua New Guinea **1975**
Malaysia **1963**
India **1947**
Sri Lanka **1948**

Women and work – Ideas page

Key element

- Knowledge and understanding of change over a period of time.

Key question

- What changes in attitude and circumstances have occurred in the lives of women between 1930 and 1970?

Background

In 1930, there were few opportunities for, and considerable bias against, women having a career. The only positions available were in domestic service, nursing and menial factory and office work. The manpower shortage in World War I had enabled women to work in factories and obtain a measure of economic independence. Even then, they were paid less than men for the same job and many left when the war ended. Their proper place was thought to be in the home and, once married, few women continued to work outside the home.

The introduction of modern electrical appliances in the 1930s helped to ease the burden of managing a home, but traditional views prevailed. World War II rekindled the necessity for women to work in factories while the men joined up. However, traditional attitudes returned once more with the ending of hostilities.

During the 1960s and 70s, these traditional attitudes came under scrutiny. Women began to demand equal pay and equal opportunities. The government supported such views with the passing of the Equal Pay Act and legislation against sex discrimination in 1975. Despite these measures and generally changing attitudes, women still remain under-represented in many walks of commercial and political life.

1940s

1950s

1970s

Activities

- The children could arrange the pictures in chronological order before answering the questions. The questions should encourage them to think about the changing attitudes to women.
- Discuss with them who does what in their home. Who does most of the cooking, washing, driving and so on? What are the reasons for this? Do they think this is a fair way for the work to be done? Are girls and boys treated any differently in school? How could things be made fairer?
- Ask the children to collect pictures from recent magazines that show men and women. What sort of things are the men/women doing? Why do you think that the men are doing some things and the women other things?
- Look through classroom history books (of any period). How many pictures of women are there? Why should this be the case?

Writing

- Children can be encouraged to interview their mother and grandmother, asking what it was like when they were younger. How have things changed for them in their way of life?

© Folens (not copiable)

The changing lives of women

These three pictures come from different times after 1940.

● Which one comes from the 1940s, which from the 1950s and which from the 1970s? What makes you think that?

● What is happening in each picture?

● What does this tell you about what women were expected to do?

● Do you think that this shows that things have got better or worse for women?

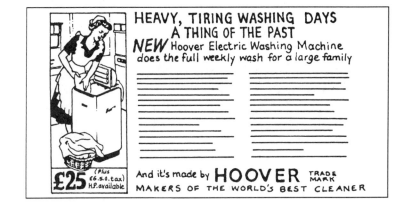

 ● Look at this table about women working.

Women workers as a percentage of all workers in a type of job				
Type of job	1931	1951	1961	1971
Owners and managers	32%	35%	35%	35%
Salespeople and shop assistants	37%	51%	54%	59%
Skilled workers	21%	15%	13%	13%
Unskilled workers	15%	20%	22%	37%
Women as a percentage of the work force	29%	30%	32%	36%

● What has changed in the sorts of jobs women had between 1931 and 1971? What has remained roughly the same?

Changes in work – Ideas page

Key element

- Knowledge and understanding of the changes that have taken place in industry since the 1930s.

Key question

- What are the main changes in British industry since the 1930s?

Background

Britain was the world's leading industrial power in the 1800s and early 1900s. Then the United States of America and Germany began to catch up and overtake. By the 1930s Britain had lost its pre-eminent position in the world and, with the collapse of the world economy in the 1930s, slipped even further behind.

One of the characteristics of employment in Britain since the 1930s has been the reduction of manpower needed in 'primary industries' (extraction, such as coal mining) and 'secondary industries' (manufacturing, such as shipbuilding). This has been caused by labour-saving technology and foreign competition. However, there has also been a steady growth in 'tertiary industries' (services, such as shops).

The main effects of a declining industry are high unemployment and less money to spend. This harms shops and other businesses as less is bought. People move away to find work, and the area becomes less attractive to new industry. A downward spiral of economic depression is the result.

Unemployment in the 1930s

Activities

- Using the pictures on the activity page, the children should identify the changes in technology and that the number of men required to install telephone cables is fewer. In the first picture the drum with cable was pulled manually. In the second, the drum was pulled on wheels. In the third, technology had advanced so much that the drum and cable were very much smaller, and easily transported.
- Explain that the following industries were the most important in 1930s Britain. How many of the children's parents work in them today?
  shipbuilding, coal mining, making iron and steel, working in cotton factories, railways
- Newer industries began to appear in the 1930s. How many of their parents work in these today?
  electrical industry, chemical industry, motor car industry
- Handled with care, a survey of parents' current jobs can be done for comparative purposes.
- The children could make a large outline map of the British Isles with the traditional centres for coal mining, shipbuilding and cotton manufacturing marked. If these industries began to disappear what would be the effect for these places?

Assembly line (making jotters)

- Explain to the children what an assembly line is. Organise them into teams to make jotters for rough work. Specify the size and number of pages for the jotters, giving them large pieces of paper and scissors. Allow them 10 minutes to make 20 jotters. Review the teams when the time is up.
- Who got the task done? What were the best ways of getting it done? Is an assembly line faster than making the whole thing yourself? Why?

Writing

- Consider the changes that have occurred in industry, and for which group or individuals they are bad or good.

© Folens (not copiable)

Changes in industry

Look at the three illustrations taken from photographs of men laying telephone cable.

● What changes can you see in the illustrations?
● Can you explain those changes?
● What does this mean for the types of jobs that have disappeared?

1914

1957

1976

● You have been told the factory you are working in is going to be automated. You will no longer have a job. What would you write in a letter to your Member of Parliament to try to stop this happening?

The use of cars since 1930 – Ideas page

Key element

- Knowledge and understanding of the growth of car travel since 1930 and the results of this.

Key questions

- Why are cars so popular?
- What problems have they caused?

Activities

- After completing the graph, use the picture on the activity page to discuss issues such as demolishing homes, noise and pollution. Compare the picture with any controversial road schemes in the local area.
- Cars are blamed for a marked drop in the quality of children's lives. Worries about safety mean they have a more restricted childhood than their parents or grandparents, who played more street games and rode bicycles in a safer environment. Ask the children to design safety posters showing the problems cars cause for them.
- Research and make a collection of car advertisements, such as the one shown opposite. Discuss the way that cars have changed in style, but also talk about the the advertisements themselves and the language that they use.

Background

Britain has been called the Great Car Economy. Car numbers have increased by an average of 10 per cent a year for the last 40 years, at the expense of public transport. In 1930 there were 32 345 km of railway line. By 1992, this had fallen to 16 528 km. Much of this was cut by Dr Beeching, chairman of British Rail in 1961, to streamline and modernise the railways to meet the challenge of road transport. In 1938 bicycle use, measured in billions of kilometres travelled, was almost the same as car use. By 1993 it was a tiny proportion.

Cars have always been controversial. Construction of the M25 around London began in 1975. It took 12 years to complete the circuit, which was 188 kilometres in length. It was built to take 85 000 vehicles a day, but by 1991 it was common to record twice as many travelling on the road.

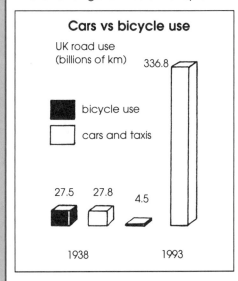

Cars vs bicycle use

UK road use (billions of km)

- ■ bicycle use
- □ cars and taxis

336.8

27.5   27.8   4.5

1938   1993

Writing

- List the advantages and disadvantages of travelling by car, bicycle and train. Complete a chart such as the one below. Ask the children to think about speed, time, safety, pollution, the efficient use of resources and health.

Transport	Advantages	Disadvantages
Car	1. Able to travel from door to door 2. 3.	

MORRIS MINOR 1000

Now better than ever

Cars and roads

- Use the figures in the table below to complete the graph.
- Mark on the figures with a dot. Join the dots to make a line graph.
- When was the smallest rise in car numbers? Why?

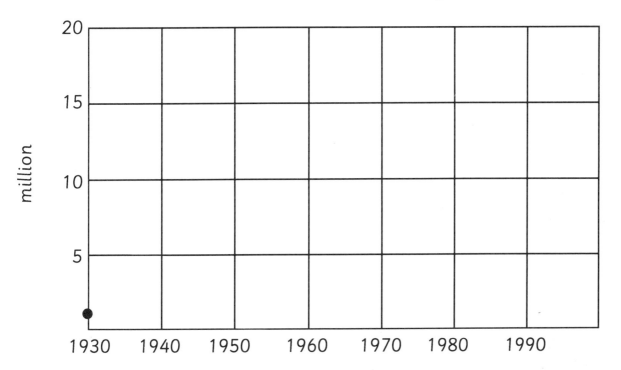

Year	Number of Cars
1930	1 million
1939	2 million
1950	2.25 million
1955	3.75 million
1960	5 million
1965	8 million
1970	10 million
1980	14.75 million
1985	16.5 million
1990	19.75 million
1993	20.1 million

Look at the picture above of a flyover built in London in 1970.
- What problems has this caused for local people? Are there any advantages for them?

Key element

- Understanding that the past constantly undergoes reinterpretation.

Key question

- Why does the past get changed by people living in the present?

Background

Many people think of the 1930s as a time of depression and despair involving marching armies of unemployed, terrible living conditions, strikes and social dislocation. What is often forgotten is that the same period saw rising living standards and technological development. The experiences of different individuals and groups tend to stamp their mark on the whole period. Sometimes the images can clash as people use history for their own purposes. For example, the 1930s are also seen as a time of certainties, good neighbourliness and a period when craftsmen produced quality products. These images are often employed by manufacturers of food and drink products to sell their goods. In such advertisements they are reinventing the past and rewriting our view of periods of the past.

Activities

- The activity page includes some fictitious advertisements that resemble real ones used today. The children could explain the attraction of each and then suggest how accurately each portrays the 1930s. Find photos of the period for comparison.
- The advertisements should help the children to see how and why the past is used in particular ways. They give a rosy view of the 1930s, presenting a comfortable, cosy time with people who were well-dressed and had plenty to eat. It is intended for the consumer to associate these elements with the products, making them more appealing. It is important to remember that advertisers are trying to persuade the public to buy the products. The children could identify other advertisements on television or in magazines that use a 1930s setting. A collection of such material can make an effective display.
- The children could create a table such as the one below, which sets out positive and negative aspects of life in the 1930s and the present. Topics could include medicine, safety in the streets, unemployment, food, entertainment, schools and family values.

living in the 1930s		living in the 1990s	
good	bad	good	bad
You could play in the streets Family values	Unemployment	Better medicine Television	More guns More cars

Writing

- Organise the children into pairs. Each pair should tell each other a special memory. Each child should then write down their partner's story. The children could then check any differences with their partners. How did these changes occur? When you tell someone else's story it is usually less vivid. Some detail has to be invented either because it was not initially told or because the listener has forgotten.

 © Folens (not copiable)

Is this what the 1930s were really like?

These are modern advertisements, with scenes from the 1930s
- What do these adverts make the 1930s look like?
- How might they help sell the things advertised?
- Why do they make the 1930s look like this?

An old lady's memory

- Why does she think the 1930s were a good time?
- Does this mean there was no crime in the 1930s?
- Do you think the fact that she was a child during the 1930s might affect her memories of the 1930s?

The changes in housing – Ideas page

Key element

- To compare, contrast and draw implications about the changes in housing.

Key question

- What changes have occurred in homes from the 1930s up to today?

Activities

- The activity page shows a middle class home in 1930. The children could identify the different features and compare them with homes today.
- Ask them to categorise types of change on a table such as the one featured on this page.
- They could identify other categories under which to make comparisons, using other sources to develop this activity.
- Using this information, they could make timelines or sequencing cards to test each other.
- They could research different house styles, using the local library.

Writing

- Ask the children to consider the changes that have taken place in our homes since the 1930s. Which do they think are the best? Why? What would they miss most if they were sent back to the 1930s?

Background

After World War I, Britain embarked on removing slum property and building decent houses for people to live in. By 1939, the housing programme had been so successful that, despite the Depression and continued growth of population, Britain had a housing surplus, although thousands of homes were still classified as slum properties.

Many households could afford a radio and a coal fire. Electrical appliances, and particularly electric lighting, made homes both clean and light and easier to maintain. Nevertheless, as many writers and social investigators were to comment, Britain was still a country of wide contrasts. The north of England, Scotland and Wales suffered the most from the decline of traditional industries (see page 10), and it was no surprise that these were also the areas of the poorest living conditions.

Old advertisements such as this can be a useful resource.

Changes in our homes

	then	now
entertainment		
heating	coal fires	
lighting		
furniture		

What has changed?

● Look at this picture of a living room in a 1930s home.

● In the space below draw some of the objects as they look today.

 ● Compare the outsides of 1930s houses with houses built today.

Housing conditions –

Key elements

- Knowledge and understanding of housing conditions in the 1930s.
- The use of pictures and building plans as sources for historical enquiry.

Key questions

- What were housing conditions like for the poor in pre-war Britain?
- How were these improved by council housing programmes?

Background

After World War I the government promised 'homes fit for heroes'. In 1919, it estimated that over 600 000 houses were needed to alleviate the chronic problems of substandard dwellings and overcrowding. Many people had no bathrooms, or even their own water supply. Dry closet toilets were still common. Local authorities were given powers to clear slum properties, build quality new houses and levy a rate to subsidise rents.

From the 1920s onwards, extensive council estates became a feature of British towns. The design of homes and estates could be uniform and drab, but they gave most tenants a vast improvement in living standards. Building was interrupted by World War II, but resumed in the 1940s and 50s. However, by the late 1960s ten percent of homes still had no bathroom.

Writing

- Ask the children to write descriptions of the new house as if they were estate agents trying to sell it. Look at the property pages of a local paper as a guide to style.
- Write a letter from the mother of the family in the picture to her sister in Blackpool, describing the pleasures and problems of moving into their new home.
- Ask the children to imagine that they lived with their families in one room, like the family in the picture. Can they make a list of problems that might come with such an arrangement?

The problems of living in one room.

1. I can never be on my own.
2. It is always cramped.
3. We all have to go to bed at the same time.

Activities

- The drawing on the activity page is based on a photograph of a slum dwelling in North Shields in the 1930s. Discuss why such indoor photos are very rare (inadequate camera technology, the shame of residents at living in such conditions, and so on). When and why do we take photos of the inside of our homes today? How useful will they be to historians in the future?
- Ask the local planning department or archives to supply you with plans of houses near your school. These could be compared with the plan on the activity page.
- Ask the children to make a pictoral survey of types of council housing in your area, for example 1920s mock-Tudor and 1960s high rise flats.
- This picture is of a girl from the 1930s, collecting water from a tap near her house. Ask the children where they collect their water from, and what it is used for. Ask them to imagine life with only an outside water tap. How many times a day would they have to go to the tap? What for?

IDEAS BANK – *Britain Since 1930*   © Folens (not copiable)

A new home

This poor family lived in one room in a crowded street, built in Victorian times. When it was knocked down in 1936 they moved into a new council house.

● How big was the family? What problems would they have had living in one room?

This is a plan of the council house.

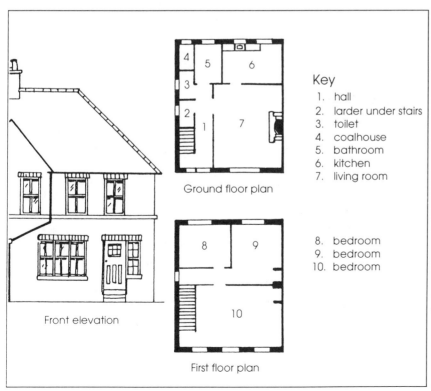

Key
1. hall
2. larder under stairs
3. toilet
4. coalhouse
5. bathroom
6. kitchen
7. living room

8. bedroom
9. bedroom
10. bedroom

Ground floor plan

Front elevation

First floor plan

● How could the family set out the furniture in their new home?
● They will have more space than before. List any new furniture that they might buy. Remember that this is 1936, so the list would not be the same as today.
● On the back of this sheet draw the plan with the furniture in place.
● How would the family have felt in their new home?

© Folens (copiable page)

Key elements

- Knowledge and understanding of life on the dole in the 1930s.
- Using contemporary documents for historical enquiry.

Key question

- What was the standard of living like for the unemployed in the 1930s?

Activities

- Explain the table on the activity page. 'Clubs' refers to saving clubs for expensive items such as Christmas presents or children's shoes. Insurance was most likely for funerals. Although the dole seems meagre, many people worked for wages of about £2 to £2.50. About one third of the population lived in poverty.
- Discuss the problems of seven people living in three rooms. What facilities would they need? It is unlikely that they had a bathroom, probably sharing an outside toilet.
- One way to save money is to cut down on unnecessary spending. Ask if any of the children are saving up for something special. Perhaps it is a little more expensive than something they would normally buy. What would they cut down on to save their money? How long would it be before they have saved enough money?

Background

Following the 1929 Wall Street Crash, the 1930s was a decade of severe unemployment, reaching a peak of almost three million (twenty per cent of the population) in January 1933.

By 1938 the rearmament programme had helped reduce this to 1.8 million. However, there was a varied picture across the country. Some areas, such as the South East, were barely affected by the Depression. They had become centres of booming new industries – motor cars or consumer electronics. Others, such as Wales and the North East, were on their knees. Their traditional industries – steel, mining and shipbuilding – were hit badly by falls in world trade, forcing many families to live on National Insurance payments.

The tables on the activity page are taken from the report of the Medical Officer for Health for the North Eastern town of Sunderland in 1934. He noted the weekly budgets of 33 families, concluding that too much of their income was required for rent and insurance, leading to malnourishment. The rate of unemployment relief caused bitter political and moral debates.

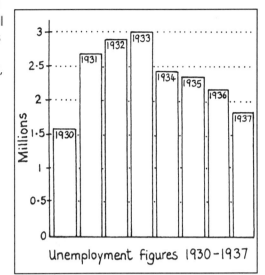

Unemployment figures 1930–1937

Writing

- Look at the column 'Other payments'. Prepare a list of items the family might need to buy every week, such as soap, or from time to time, such as bedding.
- There is no mention of entertainment of any kind. Find out whether they had any recreational activities. Ask the children to write a postcard from the oldest child to his/her grandmother.
- Using the information in the table, prepare a menu sheet for the family for one week. It might look like this:

	Monday	Tuesday	Wednesday	Thursday	Friday	Saturday	Sunday
breakfast:							
dinner:							
tea:							

Living on the dole

The parents in this family were unemployed in 1934. They had to live on National Insurance payments from the government, usually called the 'dole'. This table was recorded by their doctor.

● s = shilling, d = pence and one shilling = 12 pence

Number in family	Rent	Coal	Gas or electric	Clothes and clubs	Insurance	Other payments (not food)	Food	Total
father mother children aged 9, 7, 6, 3 and 3 months	9s	1s	1s 2d	5s	2s 10d	1s 10d soap etc	15s 2d plus 3s from grand-parents	£1 16s 2d
Today's money	45p	5p	6p	25p	14p	9p	91p	£1 95

● How many people are in this family?
● How much are they given to live on by the government?
● Look at the 'Other payments' column. What else might they need to buy besides soap?
● The family doctor was worried about the way this family had to live. Suggest two reasons why.

● Look at the food table.
● Using the table, plan three different meals for a family of two adults and two children. How much would each meal cost?

Food table	old money s	old money d	new money p
meat	3	0	15
flour	2	71/2	13
yeast	0	1/2	1
milk (tins)	0	91/2	4
sugar	1	3	6
potatoes	0	8	31/2
greens	0	5	2
butter	1	5	7
bacon	0	11	41/2
lard	0	5	2
tea	1	4	7
cocoa	0	10	4
eggs	1	0	5
onions	0	3	1
baking powder	0	2	1
jam	0	61/2	3
salt	0	1	01/2
pepper	0	1	01/2
rice	0	3	1
gravy salt	0	1	01/2
sago	0	4	2
milk	1	6	71/2
Total	18	2	91

Make an Anderson shelter – Ideas page

Key element

- Knowledge and understanding of the effects of air warfare on the Home Front.

Key questions

- What was it like to live in a time when people were bombed?
- What was it like to live inside an Anderson shelter?

Writing

- Why did the following items have to be inside an air raid shelter?
  - gas mask
  - identity card
  - ration book
  - first aid kit
  - torch

Background

It was widely feared, at the outbreak of World War II, that a huge number of casualties would be suffered as a consequence of bombing raids. Civilians needed cheap, mass produced air raid shelters. Sir John Anderson, the Home Secretary, ordered the production of outdoor air raid shelters, called Anderson shelters. Nearly one and a half million had been given away free by September 1939. Each one could hold six adults.

However, there were problems with the Anderson shelters. They frequently became water-logged, and you needed a garden to put them in. Fewer than one in four people had a garden, so the government came up with an indoor shelter called a Morrison shelter. This was little more than a steel mesh box with a mattress inside. It did have the advantage, however, of being able to be placed under a table.

Anderson shelter

Activities

- Talk the children through the activity page.
- Ask them to do the writing activity above.
- Now make your own Anderson shelter.
  - You will need several large cardboard boxes, preferably the sort in which egg cartons are transported, although any large sheets of plain brown card can be used.
  - Strip off the outer layer of paper to reveal the corrugated surface.
  - Paint the surface of the corrugated card silver or white.
  - Fold the card, as illustrated, and staple the back wall to the main body.
  - Fill small hessian bags or old pillowcases with sand and place them around the base to make the walls secure.
  - Cut out an entrance to the shelter and place it at the front as shown.
  - Place the shelter in the activity corner.

- Choose a small group of children (the number depends on the size of your Anderson shelter) to occupy the shelter, and role-play an air raid. Discuss how they felt in the shelter.
- Match these words with their meaning:

Words:	Meanings:
Anderson	people killed or injured
bunks	indoor shelter
casualties	
corrugated	small beds, one above the other
Morrison	garden shelter
	wavy surface

© Folens (not copiable)

An air raid

● Look at the pictures below. What do they show?

● Using what you see in the pictures, describe the night of a massive bombing raid where you live, and the damage you found in your street after the air raid the next morning.
● Describe how you felt about the bombing.
● Begin your story with the following sentences:

> Everything seemed cosy and warm that night as we lazed in front of the coal fire.
> But it was a night never to forget. Just as my eyes became heavy with sleep the siren wailed...

© Folens (copiable page)

Make a gas mask – | Ideas page

Key element

- Knowledge and understanding of the fear of gas attacks at the outbreak of World War II, and the precautions that were taken.

Key questions

- Why did everybody receive a gas mask from the government?
- What was it like for the children to carry the mask at all times?

Background

Poison gas had been used with terrible effect during World War I and many feared that gas bombs would be dropped on Britain when war was declared in 1939. Every citizen was issued with a gas mask inside a brown cardboard box, which they were expected to carry with them at all times. The children may spot these in photographs of the period.

The gas masks themselves weighed 0.5kg and contained charcoal, which soaked up the poisonous gas and let fresh air through. No gas bombs were actually used during the war, when high explosive detonated bombs could do far more damage. There are still a number of gas masks around and it is important that children do not try them on because many of them contain asbestos, now known to be a dangerous substance.

Writing

- Babies cannot wear the standard issue gas mask. Ask the children to write and draw a brief for a design for protecting babies from a gas attack.
- Give them a picture of someone wearing a gas mask (you could enlarge the one on the activity page). Ask them to label the picture, explaining how the gas mask works. Use these words (they might have to look some up in the dictionary): window, straps, poison gas, filter, rubber face piece, pure air.
- Ask them to think of problems that might occur with their masks. For example, rubber is very tight, how could they stretch it? The window might get steamed up – how would you stop this from happening? (Think about what you might do to stop goggles misting over.)

Activities

- Before asking the children to make the replica gas mask on the activity page, ensure that there is no-one with breathing difficulties or who suffers from claustrophobia.
- Ask them what it feels like to wear it, and how it might affect them if they had to carry it with them at all times. Would it hamper their movements, for example during sports activities? What if they lost their gas mask? They could make a list of any problems that might be experienced.

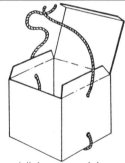

- The children could go on to make a case to hold their mask.
- Ask them to write instructions on using the mask. Where would they place the instructions?
- The final activity shows a poster designed to warn people to always carry a gas mask. Ask the children to design and illustrate their own poster.

    © Folens (not copiable)

Make a gas mask

- Follow these instructions to make a gas mask.
1. Roll some black sugar paper into a cone shape.
2. Trim the wide end so that it fits comfortably on your face.
3. Attach strips of 10cm wide sugar paper to make straps.
4. Fold the cone gently and cut out a square section to see through. Stick cellophane over this hole.
5. Paint a yoghurt pot or paper cup black and make holes in the base. Tape the cup over the end of the cone.

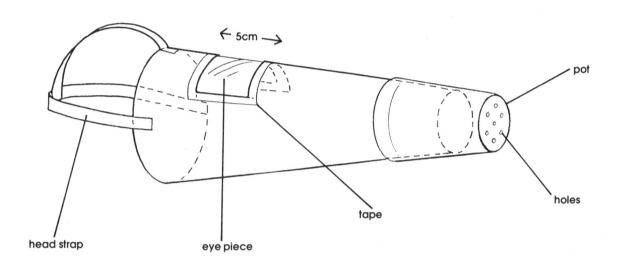

← 5cm →

pot

holes

tape

head strap

eye piece

- Wear your gas mask. How does it feel? Do you like it? What was it like for the people in the war who had to wear them?

- Make a carry case to hold your gas mask.

- Look at this poster. What does it aim to achieve? Design your own poster that warns people to always carry their gas masks.

Hitler will send no warning
so always carry your gas mask

© Folens (copiable page)

Bomber! – Ideas page

Key elements

- Knowledge and understanding of the significance of air warfare in World War II.
- Knowledge of different types of aircraft used for war in World War II

Key question

- How did Germany launch bombing raids against Britain?

Background

If the most important weapon of World War I was the machine gun, in World War II it was the aeroplane, as this invention changed the nature of warfare in the twentieth century. Before hostilities broke out it was widely believed that the bomber alone could make the enemy submit. It was this belief, and the easy victories that the *Luftwaffe* (German air force) had enjoyed up to 1940, that persuaded Hitler to pursue this course of action.

During the Battle of Britain the *Luftwaffe* concentrated on bombing fighter airfields in the South East of England, as a preparation for a seaborne invasion. When invasion plans were abandoned they switched to bombing London and other cities by night. This was known as the 'Blitz'. By 1942, the tide of the war had begun to turn and a mass bombing of Germany began. The Royal Air Force was joined in this task by Americans based in Britain. Nevertheless, the German bombing of major British cities and industries continued throughout the war.

Activities

- The children should look at the examples of different aircraft that were used in World War II and identify the types that would be suitable for particular tasks. This will give them an idea of how the war was faught, and how the Home Front in particular were affected by the use of aeroplanes (bombers) in conflict.
- Larger versions of the silhouette aircraft can be drawn using an overhead projector. These can be pinned to the ceiling. Members of the class can use the silhouettes for aircraft recognition.
- The activity on page 29 is a simulation of a German bombing raid on Britain. The instructions for the activity are on page 28.
- A larger version of the map can be produced using an overhead projector. Use the same number of aircraft and anti-aircraft guns as described in the instructions. In this case, however, the aircraft can only move one square at a time.
- The co-ordinates must be reported back to the British and German bases accurately. If they are not, the aircraft remains where it is until the next round. One child can act as official observer and determine whether the co-ordinates given are the accurate ones.
- This activity will give the children a good basic knowledge of co-ordinates, and might be linked with other subjects such as maths and geography. The word 'co-ordinates' will have to be explained to the children if they have not used the term before. The method of obtaining co-ordinates may also have to be explained:
  - horizontal line first = letters
  - vertical axis second = numbers
  - possible co-ordinates could be G10, L14 and so on.

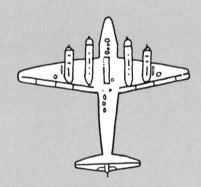

Writing

- Creative writing could be done on the following:
  - What would it be like to fly on a German mission over Britain?
  - How would you feel as enemy aircraft and anti-aircraft guns blasted and rocked the aircraft you were in?
  - What do you feel for the people below who will be bombed?
  - Has anyone in your family been bombed? If so, write about their experiences.

World War II aircraft

Look at these aircraft.
- Which would you send to stop German bombers?
- Which aircraft would you use to take British troops overseas?
- Which would the Germans use for fighting in the air?

Hawker Hurricane – British fighter

North American Mustang – British/American fighter

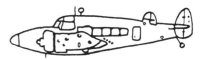

Hudson III – British coastal patrol

Supermarine spitfire – British fighter

Junkers Ju 88 – German bomber

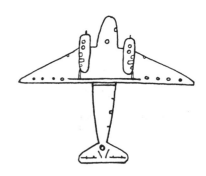

Douglas Dakota – British/American transport

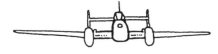

Messerschmitt Me 110 – German fighter

Dornier D0127 – German bomber

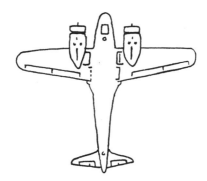

Avro Anson – British coastal patrol/trainer

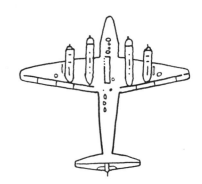

Focke-wulf Fw 200 – German bomber

- What is the difference between a fighter and a bomber?

© Folens (copiable page)   IDEAS BANK – *Britain Since 1930*

Bomber!

1.
- One player is in charge of British Command.
- The other player is in charge of German Command.

2.
- Three German aircraft begin in Norway and three in France.
- Three British aircraft begin in Scotland and three in England.

3.
- German Command must write their target cities down but not tell the other player. They cannot change their targets during the course of the exercise.

4.
- In turns, spin a coin.
  heads aircraft moves one square in any direction
  tails aircraft moves two squares in any direction

5.
- If aircraft land on the same square then the player who spins a head wins the battle in the skies.
- The losing aircraft is removed from the board.

6.
- At each British city there is an anti-aircraft battery – powerful artillery that could shoot bombers out of the sky.
- When an aircraft lands on a city square a coin is spun twice. If the same side comes up both times then the bomber is shot out of the sky. If this happens the aircraft is removed from the board.
  If not, the German bomber manages to release his bombs and the aircraft can return home at a faster speed:

  heads   three moves
  tails   two moves

Log Book

During the exercise British Command must keep a record of what happens to all of the aircraft.

- What happens to the British aircraft?
- What happens to the German aircraft?

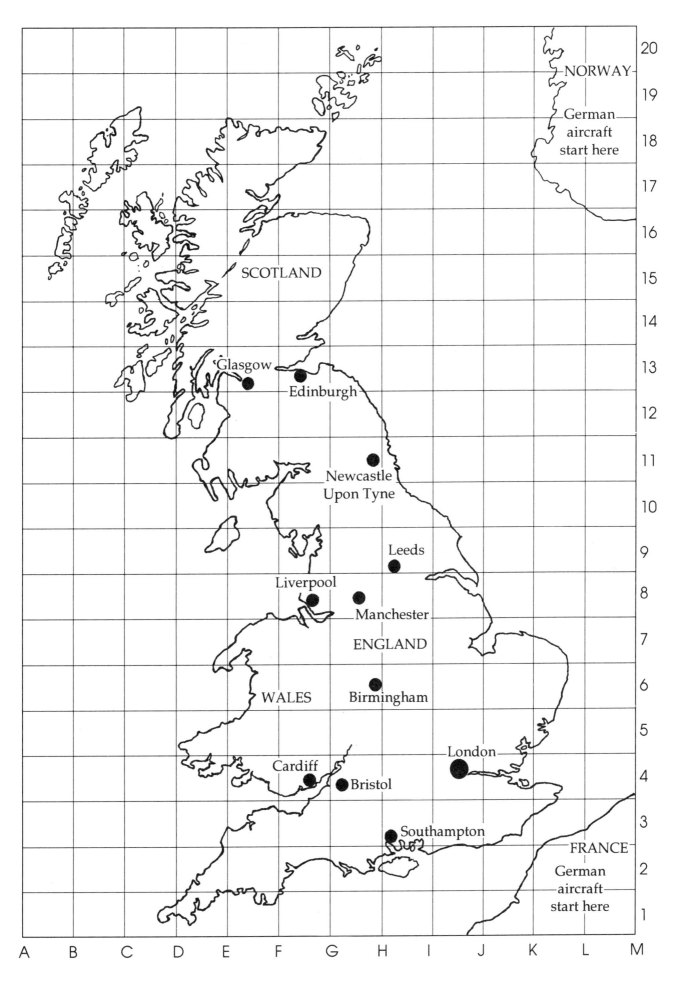

20
NORWAY
19
German
aircraft
start here
18

17

16

SCOTLAND
15

14

Glasgow
13
Edinburgh

12

Newcastle
11
Upon Tyne

10

Leeds
9

Liverpool
Manchester
8

ENGLAND
7

Birmingham
6
WALES

London
5

Cardiff
Bristol
4

3
Southampton
FRANCE
German
aircraft
start here
2

1

A B C D E F G H I J K L M

Evacuation – | Ideas page |

Key element

- Knowledge and understanding of evacuation during World War II.

Key questions

- Why were children evacuated during World War II?
- What was it like for them?

Activities

- Discuss the feelings of children placed in homes in safe areas. The activity page includes some examples of the people that took in evacuees.
- The children should imagine what it would have been like and write a postcard home describing their experiences in the countryside. Some evacuees might have felt unhappy. The children may not want to worry their poorly mother. How might they choose their words so she is not upset?
- On this page there is an example of World War II government propaganda. It is a poster that discourages mothers from trying to take back their evacuated children. Discuss with the children how the population were encouraged to do as the government wished. Have them design and draw a poster which encourages mothers to evacuate their children.

Background

More than 3 500 000 people had left their homes for safer areas even before war was declared. To prevent children being killed by bombing raids, it was decided that they should be evacuated to rural areas. They all had to be housed. Volunteers went to safe areas, checking on who had room in their homes. They were not allowed to refuse to take an evacuee.

Local people tried to pick the children they wanted. Some children settled in quickly while others became desperately homesick. Evacuation often proved a shock to both parties. Inner city children arrived with their one and only set of clothes, often infected with lice and fleas. Some ate with their hands, others were unsure of what a bed was for and slept on the floor. Some children ran back to their mothers. In other instances mothers asked to have their children back. By 1940, nearly all of the evacuees had been reunited with their families.

Writing

- Give the children other characterisations to imagine and write about:

John Handy (farmer)
I'm not a wealthy man and yet the government says I must take in these little runts from the city. More mouths to feed and those hungry city kids'll eat me out of house and home if I'm not careful. Don't want no idle chattering girls. Big, strong lad to help me in the fields. Plenty of fresh air'll keep the lad healthy and busy so he can pay his way.

Mr and Mrs Welcome (Sea View Hotel owners)
H'mm we'll have to be careful we don't end up with any bedwetters, washing sheets all the time. Not now that we've only got a handful of guests because the war's on. Well-behaved ones who don't wander down to the beach – now it's all mined in case the Germans land. Heaven knows we need the money now – not that it's generous. Just enough to give them the simplest of foods.

- The children could enact the different parts, playing either the evacuees or the people who take them in. What happens when they arrive? What do they have to do when they get there? What are the people like?

TAKE THEM BACK! TAKE THEM BACK!

DON'T do it Mother

LEAVE THE CHILDREN WHERE THEY ARE

Away from home in the war

- Imagine you have been sent away from home to keep you safe from bombing raids.
- Choose one of the descriptions of the people below and write a postcard home telling them what life is like in your new home.

The first thing we'll have to do is to examine their hair and no doubt burn their clothes. These poor, unfortunate city children are bound to have lice and fleas. Must keep them out of mischief. My butler and housekeeper will see that they have no time for trouble and are kept out of the way when I have important guests staying at the manor house. Besides it'll be good training for them – learning how to do the servants' work.

I must say I'm looking forward to having children about the house. Cottage seems so empty since my dear hubby passed on and the rooms are so silent like. Never had children of my own and there's those poor loves suffering all that bombing and next to no food and far away from their mums. I'll be their mum so they'll not want for anything.

POST CARD

CORRESPONDENCE

ADDRESS ONLY

© Folens (copiable page)

Knitting for the troops – Ideas page

Key element

- Knowledge of the range of activities to support the war effort on the Home Front.

Key question

- In what ways did citizens team together to help the war effort?

Writing

- Pretend you are the member of a knitting circle during the war. Write a letter to the soldier who you hope will make use of the woollen wristlet you have knitted.
- Pretend you are the soldier who has received the wristlet. Write a reply to the person sending the woollen wristlet.

Background

Almost every citizen felt it to be their patriotic duty to help the effort to win the war. One such co-operative venture consisted of groups of women who banded together to form knitting circles. On the activity page is an illustration of a photograph from 1939, of a knitting circle in Newcastle upon Tyne. The aim of the photograph was to show that everyone, in one way or another, was making an effort to help to win the war. Whether these garments were actually worn by the soldiers on the front is debatable. The real importance of such efforts was in giving everyone a sense of contribution.

Activities

- Ask the children to look carefully at the picture of the women knitting and answer the questions on the activity page.
- Those who are able could use the pattern provided to knit the wristlet. A wristlet is similar to the wrist bands used in sport, only they were used to keep the soldiers warm.
- What other types of woollen garments could be easily knitted for the troops?
- What other activities could people take part in to help the war effort?

Activity	How it would be organised	How it would help
Collecting paper to recycle		

- Discuss the word 'morale'. Why was it important to keep morale high in the war? What sort of things could be done to keep people's morale high?
- The wristlets knitting pattern is featured below. If any of the children can knit, they could make a pair of their own.

Wristlets Knitting Pattern

1 oz. 2-ply angora or cashmere wool.
3 No. 12 needles – points at both ends.

To obtain the best results, it is essential that you use the exact materials mentioned above.

Cast on 48 sts. on to 3 needles – 16 on each.
1st round – K. 2. P. 2. Continue to end round.
2nd round – K. 2. P. 2. Continue to end round.
Work in K. 2. P. 2 ribbing until wristlets measure $4\frac{1}{2}$in. in length.
Cast off.
(Tension should be 12 rows to 1 in. in depth.)
Length $4\frac{1}{2}$in.

Knitting for the troops

This picture is like a photograph that was taken for a
newspaper in 1939.
- What is happening in the photograph?
- Why did these people get together to knit?
- What sorts of things could they be making?

Here are two items that people knitted to send to the troops.
- Write why you think soldiers needed these things.

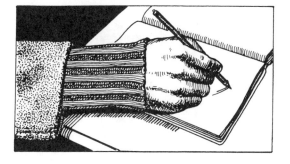

_____
_____
_____
_____
_____
_____
_____

- Think of ways that you would help people who
  were away from home fighting in the war.

Key element

- To understand the system of rationing during World War II.

Key question

- Why were food and clothing rationed during World War II?

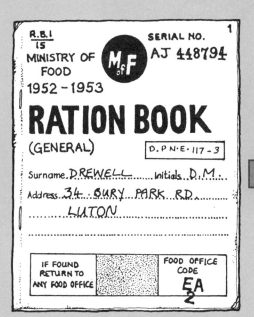

Background

Every family in the land was affected by the war. Husbands were frequently away fighting, and so the responsibility fell upon the mother of the family to tend and protect the children. The first concern of most mothers was to obtain enough for their families to eat. Britain relied heavily on imported foods, which were vulnerable to German submarine attack. As a result, many foods were in short supply.

Rationing was introduced so that any food and clothing might be shared fairly. In January 1940 everyone was issued with a ration book. Every time you bought sugar, bacon, milk and clothes you also gave the shopkeeper some coupons. By 1941, meat, tea and jam were added to the ration list. All foods were given points by the government, and each adult was allowed 16 points of food per week. Each child was allocated 12 points. People grumbled, but they were prepared to put up with this because they felt it was fair. In fact, through rationing, poorer people had a better diet than they had before the war.

Some people bought and sold things on the 'black market' to avoid the restrictions. This was against the law, and if you were caught you could be fined or imprisoned.

Activities

- The game on the activity page is to help the children to understand the limited amount of food available, and how carefully mothers spent their coupons.
- Once the children are familiar with the game, put a time limit on it.
- When the game is over they should look at their cards and plan their meals.

- Find a ration book and use it to answer the following questions:
  - What information does it give?
  - Why did you have to say which shop you were going to buy your food from?
  - What does this tell us about how people shopped? Were there lots of cars to take you to other shops? Were there supermarkets where you could buy everything under one roof?
- Ask the children how many points they would have for two adults and three children. What would they buy? How long would items last before they had to buy them again?
- Find out how many of the rationed items your family uses in a week. What is the difference between what you eat now and what was allowed during wartime?

Writing

- Ask the children to write a letter to the local rationing office about their grandmother, who is living with them. She has fallen ill and needs extra food. She needs to have better foods, such as milk, cheese and meats, to build up her strength. How would they persuade the office to allow more rations for her?

Rationing

1. Make five copies of the cards, cut them out, shuffle them and place them on the 'cards' squares. Make sure that each shop has a sold out card or bonus cards.

2. You have ten minutes to collect as many food points as possible for a family of two adults and two children. For one week's food, each adult is allowed 16 points and each child 12 points.

3. Take it in turns to roll two dice and move that number of squares. If you land on a shop you can take one card. If you pick up a sold out card you miss a turn (return it to the bottom of the pile). You can move in any direction to try to collect food cards.

4. At the end of ten minutes, add up your points. Bonus points can be used for any food. Will your family be hungry? Will they have had a good diet?

2 D	3 G	3 G	2 C	3 G	3 B	3 B	2 G	SORRY,	LOSE	1	2
3 PINTS OF MILK	225g JAM	55g TEA	30g CHEESE	225g SUGAR	115g BACON	55g MEAT	170g BUTTER	SOLD OUT	1 POINT	BONUS POINT	BONUS POINTS

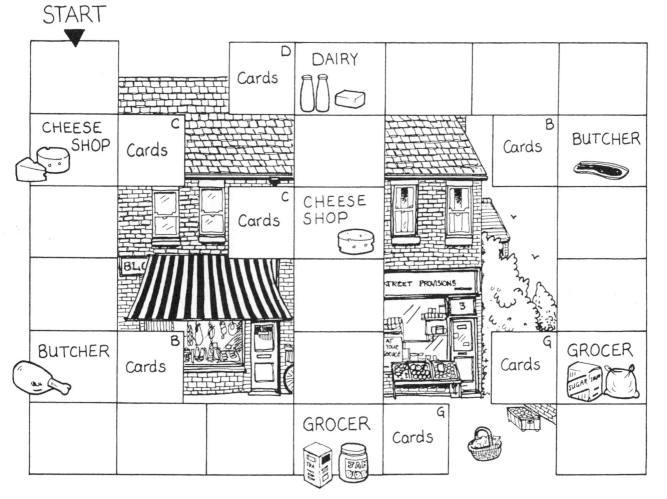

START

© Folens (copiable page)

Working women in World War II – Ideas page

Key element

- Knowledge and understanding of women at work in World War II.

Key questions

- How were women recruited for war work?
- What prejudice did they face in the workplace?

Activities

- Discuss the difference in views towards women shown in the two sources on the activity page. The cartoon gives a light-hearted view of resentment towards women on the shopfloor, but is typical of the sarcasm that many routinely faced. Yet it is double-edged – the man is reacting to a threat while the woman is lifting the weights. The children might ask why he is not helping her.
- Ask the children to research and display pictures of women at work or in the services. Try to find a wide range of women's roles that were not traditionally female, such as operating radar and anti-aircraft guns, welding and crane driving.
- Read out Bevin's comment on women and the war. Discuss the importance of mass production in modern warfare, and what might have happened if women had not gone to work.

Background

By June 1944 about a third of men of working age were in the services. The resulting labour shortage was met by women. Around 7 500 000 women were conscripted into war work, while 500 000 volunteered for the forces. Their role in industries such as munitions, aircraft production and steel manufacturing was vital. Women also worked in the fields in the 'Women's Land Army'. Ernest Bevin, the Minister of Labour, was to comment, 'Our women tipped the scales of war', but the opinions of many in the workplace were mixed.

The cartoon on the activity page points to common prejudices of male workers – that women were not capable of tackling industrial jobs or that employers might use them as a source of cheap labour. Little was done to promote equal pay, although many women demonstrated that they could master highly-skilled jobs in months rather than the years required in a traditional apprenticeship. Usually they were confined to labouring or semi-skilled work.

In 1945 women were expected to return to their 'real role' as wives and mothers. Most of them agreed with this. There was little discussion of better opportunities in the postwar world. In the short term, however, many individual women enjoyed the companionship, independence and relatively good pay brought about by their wartime experiences. On this page is an advertisement that shows that, during the war, women were considered an important part of the workforce.

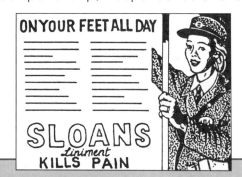

Writing

- Invite women who worked during the war to talk to the children. Prepare a list of questions such as:
  - How did the men you worked with treat you?
  - What was your boss/manager/foreman like?
  - Did you ever get into trouble?
  - Were you paid the same as a man?
  - Did you want to stay at work when the war ended?
- Record the session on tape or video, transcribe and illustrate some of the answers and send a copy to the respondent.

© Folens (not copiable)

Women and work

During the war the government ordered all unmarried women to work. Many of them went into factories making weapons, ammunitions or supplies. Others went to work on the land.

Look at the two pictures.
- How is the first meant to encourage women to work in factories?
- Why would the government want to do this?

Look at the picture on the right.
- What is happening in the cartoon? Why has the man got his eyes covered?
- Draw another cartoon with the woman talking to the man. What is she saying?

© Folens (copiable page)

Key element

- To look at food shortages and diet during World War II, using recipes as a source for historical enquiry.

Key questions

- Why was food so important to the war effort?
- How were people encouraged to make the best of shortages?

Activities

- Prepare a display of wartime rations. Do families still eat these foods today, if so in what quantities do they eat them?
- Invite parents to a wartime meal, specially prepared by the children.
- Arguably the British people eat poorer quality food now than in 1945. Discuss what foods are healthy and what foods are unhealthy. In your discussion mention things such as sugar content and the use of preservatives.
- Potato Pete was used to persuade people to eat more potatoes. Design a poster showing him recommending cold potatoes in a salad.
- Visit an allotment or vegetable garden to see what can be grown on a small patch of land.

Background

Food rationing was introduced in January 1940, and became tighter as the war progressed. It was the job of the Ministry of Food to distribute supplies and help housewives to manage. Advice centres were set up all over the country and gave demonstrations anywhere there were large groups of people – works canteens, village halls and market squares. Marguerite Patten, who worked as an adviser, remembered: 'It was our job to persuade people that they would love salad made out of raw carrots, turnips and cabbage.'

Publicity campaigns such as 'Dig for Victory' were among the most successful wartime propaganda. This emphasised that anyone who was not in the services could fight the war in the fields and the allotments. Ironically, the British people were probably better nourished during the war than at any time before or since.

Writing

- Wartime schools were encouraged to join in the 'Dig for Victory' campaign to persuade people to grow more of their own food. Show the children a copy of the poster on this page. Ask them to prepare a publicity campaign to go with it. This could include other posters, catch-phrases such as 'Mind your peas and avoid the queues', recipes, gardening tips (ask parents), and radio information broadcasts.

The kitchen front

During the war, many foods were rationed or hard to find. The Ministry of Food (with Lord Woolton in charge) gave advice on how to prepare wholesome meals.

● Try making these recipes.

Porridge Scones
250g cold porridge
125g flour
125g oatmeal
1 teaspoon bicarbonate of soda
1/2 teaspoon salt
2 teaspoons cream of tartar

Mix all the dry ingredients and work in the cold porridge. Roll or pat out to about 4cm thick and bake in a hot oven for 20 minutes.

Lord Woolton Pie
500g diced potatoes
500g cauliflower
500g carrots
500g swede
3 or 4 spring onions
1 tablespoon oatmeal
1 teaspoon vegetable extract

Cook together for ten minutes with just enough water to cover. Allow to cool. Sprinkle with parsley and cover with wholemeal pastry. Bake in a moderate oven. Serve hot with brown gravy.

● Here is a wartime radio jingle about food:
'Those who have the will to win
Cook potatoes in their skin
Knowing that the sight of peelings
Deeply hurts Lord Woolton's feelings.'

I'm an Energy Food !
Says 'POTATO PETE'

● Write a radio jingle about how good carrots are for you.

Key element

- To appreciate how and why information may be interpreted in different ways, especially in wartime.

Key question

- What is propaganda and how was it used by both sides during the war?

Activities

- Make the activity page a guessing game at first then, when the children have done it, discuss the puzzle in detail.
  - Why have pigs been chosen to resemble Hitler?
  - Why make the sheet a folding puzzle?
  - Where might the sheet have been handed out?
  - What effect is the sheet supposed to have?
- Discuss why laughter is especially important in war. Try this genuine wartime joke:
  On the farm I was busy milking and an old lady said 'Young man why aren't you at the front?' So I said, 'Nay missus, there's no milk at that end'.
- Compare the pig puzzle of Hitler with the picture on this page, or any other favourable portraits in reference books. What has the artist done to present Hitler as a hero? Where might pictures like this have been shown?

Background

The four pigs on the activity sheet fold to make a picture of Adolf Hitler. This sheet has been copied from a version that was circulated in factories and offices during World War II. The pigs present an amusing and insulting puzzle. No one knows who drew the original, but a similar version featuring Saddam Hussein appeared during the Gulf War. Sheets like this are an example of propaganda, the political advertising with which countries try to win 'the war of words'.

Propaganda is usually controlled by governments. In Germany, the population had been fed the Nazi view of events since 1933, when Hitler took power. Göebbels, head of the Ministry of Propaganda, coined the famous saying that a lie repeated a million times becomes the truth.

On the Home Front, after 1939 the Ministry of Information became the centre of British propaganda. Its most important roles were controlling information released by the media and explaining the government's policies to the people. By 1942, £200 000 a month was being spent on poster advertising – a staggering sum for the time.

Writing

- Display a collection of propaganda posters from World War II. Photocopy these from textbooks or use full size replicas such as those sold by the Imperial War Museum. Ask the children to write captions explaining how the design gets the message across. Do they always work? The British poster shown on this page, for example, has a bland and ambiguous slogan. Who were 'US' – the government, the people or both?

YOUR COURAGE
YOUR CHEERFULNESS
YOUR RESOLUTION
WILL BRING
US VICTORY

- If possible, video a collection of advertisements shown on children's television. Discuss how advertising is similar to propaganda. How are the advertisements trying to persuade people to buy the products? How are they targeting children or parents? Ask the children to write a review of an advertisement that they like or dislike, explaining the content or plot and the reasons for their opinion.

Make up the puzzle

This four-pig puzzle was drawn during World War II.
- What happens if you fold line A1 over to A2 and line B1 down to B2?
- Why do you think the artist has used pigs?

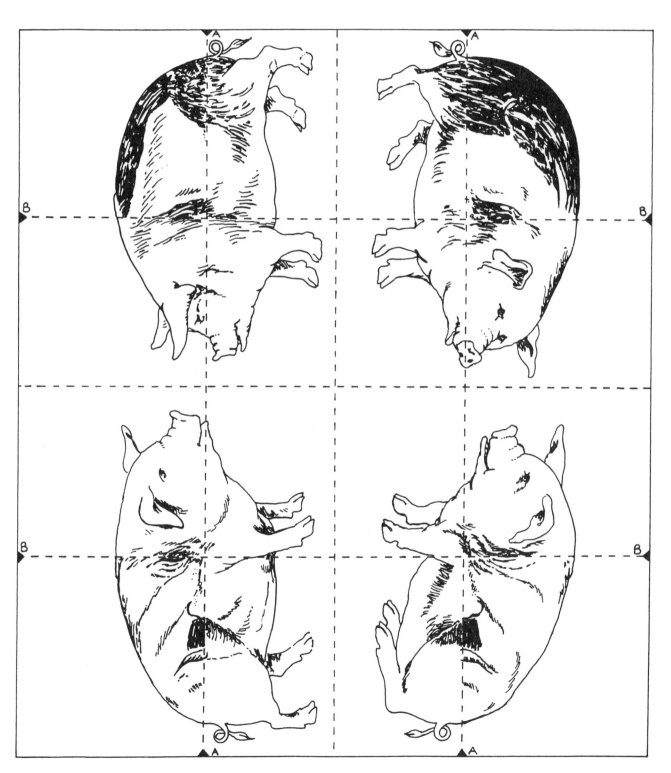

Courtesy of Lancaster City Museums

© Folens (copiable page)   IDEAS BANK – *Britain Since 1930*   41

Coronation 1953 – Ideas page

Key element

● Knowledge and understanding of the Coronation as a feature of postwar Britain. To place the reign of Queen Elizabeth II in a chronological framework.

Key questions

● Why was the Coronation so important to Britain?
● How can contemporary advertisements be used as source material?

Activities

● Ask the children to look at the design of the advertisement. Why would it especially interest people in 1953? Is this a good advertisement for such a business? Point out that the company sells reproduction furniture. What does this mean?
● Prepare a frieze comparing aspects of life in 1558 with those in 1953. The children could compare a timber-framed house with a semi, a horse and cart with a lorry, different fashions and school rooms.
● Think of another product to advertise that could be linked with Coronations, such as a televisions or jewels.

Background

The Coronation was a time of national rejoicing. It was intended to mark a fresh beginning, throwing off the austerity of the 1940s. The phrase 'the New Elizabethan Age' was coined to catch the optimism represented by a young and beautiful queen. Commentators expressed the hope that the reign of Elizabeth II would be as memorable as that of her ancestor. The family tree on the activity page deliberately highlights the two Elizabeths. It uses this to market period and contemporary furniture. Furniture styles are often named after the reigning monarch or family, such as Jacobean or Georgian.

The ancient ceremony demanded that the monarch be crowned 'in the sight of all the people' and this happened as never before. An excited crowd of over 50 000 slept in The Mall the night before, and on 2nd June the streets along the processional route were packed. More importantly, another 20 million viewers crowded around 2 500 000 television sets, many of them bought specially for the occasion.

SEE IT ALL on
TELEVISION!
'PYE' AUTOMATIC PICTURE CONTROL
T.V. TABLE MODEL   PRICE £64/18/0
'ECKO'
TABLE MODEL
PRICE £64/0/0
Blacketts
SUNDERLAND TELEPHONE: 56491

Writing

● If possible, make a display of Coronation ephemera. Use souvenirs, newspaper articles, advertisements and so on. Ask the local library and parents to help with this. Write a caption for each item.
● Use text and library books to research a timeline of furniture styles.
● How might your school celebrate the Coronation of King Charles III? Write a programme of events. This might include a bonfire and barbecue, a Coronation assembly, prayers for the new king and so on.

    © Folens (not copiable)

Coronation 1953

On 2nd June 1953, Queen Elizabeth II was crowned.
There were celebrations such as firework displays,
dances and street parties.

● Look carefully at this advertisement. What is it for?
● What does the main part of the advertisement show?
Why do you think this design was chosen in 1953?

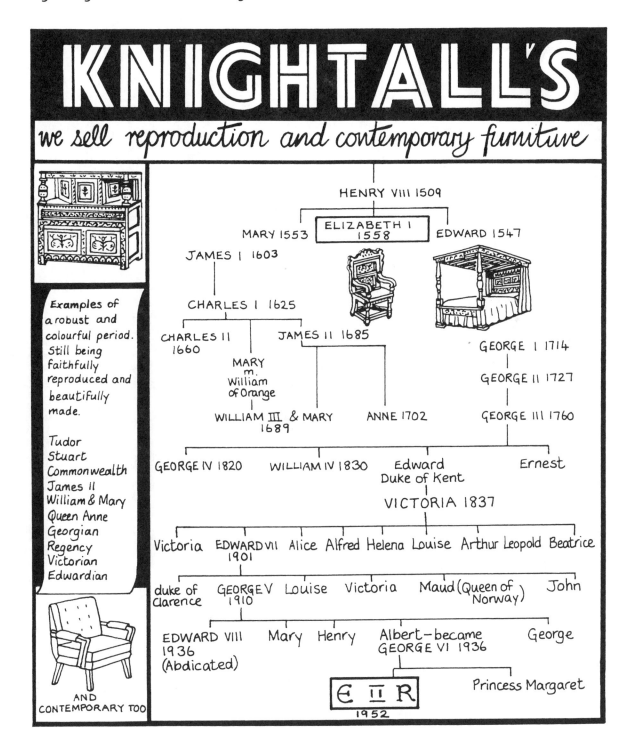

Fashion in the Sixties – Ideas page

Key elements

- To show the social diversity of youth culture in the 1960s.
- To show how fashion can be a source for historical enquiry.

Key question

- How did young people behave and dress in the 1960s?

Activities

- Discuss why young people might want to look different from their parents, even to the point of shocking them. Make a display of popular fashions amongst young people in the 1990s. What are some of the popular youth cultures now?
- Create a class Sixties Museum. This might include family photographs, advertisements, old clothes, old money, LP covers, a portable record player, magazines and newspapers.
- Set the children a research task. Use text and reference books to make a 'Sixties in the News' timeline with at least one event from each year. Copy or make up headlines for key events, such as the assassination of Kennedy, the Great Train Robbery, the Aberfan disaster or the *Torrey Canyon* running aground.

Background

The 1960s are a rich source of social history. This was a decade in which young people made the news, not least because there were so many of them. After World War II, millions of ex-servicemen and their wives decided to start families. This was called the 'baby boom' generation, and it grew up in the Sixties. It was also a time of full employment – teachers in charge of careers had only to help young people choose from the many jobs on offer. New types of freedom, notably more open attitudes towards sex, created the phrase the 'permissive society'. Fashion and music led the way. Mini skirts allowed girls to dress in a way that shocked older people. The Beatles' LP *Sergeant Pepper's Lonely Hearts Club Band* marked the arrival of psychedelic music, exploring different ways of perceiving reality. It also illustrated the increasing impact of drug culture on mainstream society.

Only a minority of young people went wholeheartedly into any of the three youth cultures shown on the activity page. Most teenagers respected their parents, went to school and worried about getting a good job. However, the trends set by these groups became part of mainstream culture. By 1967 bells and beads were on sale in Woolworths.

Writing

- Parents and grandparents may be a rich source of oral history for the 1960s. Prepare a questionnaire that they can answer at home. Focus on fashions, favourite groups, TV programmes and news events. Break the answers down for a themed display on one subject, such as Pop Music. Look out for views that show disapproval of Sixties culture.

© Folens (not copiable)

Fashion in the Sixties

Young people in the 1960s had more freedom and money than ever before, but teenagers were not all the same. Different groups had their own styles of dress, favourite music and ways of behaving.

- Use these three models to make your own Sixties fashion gallery. Cut them out and make a display. Label each one.
- Use the word lists, and any extra research you can do, to write captions to go alongside them.

Rockers

- black leather jackets
- jeans
- motor bikes
- greased hair
- rock 'n' roll music
- hated Mods

Hippies

- flower children
- face paint
- colourful, second-hand clothes
- scruffy
- bells and beads
- long hair
- sandals
- believed in love and peace
- some took drugs
- kaftans
- Indian music

Mods

- smart
- new neat suits
- short hair, blow waved or back combed
- Italian scooters covered with lamps or badges
- suede shoes
- favourite band The Who
- hated Rockers

Key element

- To identify positive features of the cultural and ethnic diversity of modern Britain.

Key questions

- What are the benefits of being a multicultural nation?
- What evidence is there of different cultures around us?
- How has foreign travel broadened tastes?

Background

Since 1945 British eating habits have been transformed. A major influence has been the impact of groups of immigrants. Greek, Italian, Chinese and Indian restaurants and take-aways have become a welcome feature of most towns. A survey in 1976 showed pizza to be Britain's favourite 'foreign' food, closely followed by chow mein and sweet and sour pork. The market for new foods was helped by growing prosperity. People could afford to go on holiday abroad and returned with more adventurous tastes. Eating out became more popular and is the fastest growing leisure activity of the 1990s. Items of produce formerly considered exotic are now a standard part of home cooking for many. This has encouraged retailers to carry ever larger stocks of foreign foodstuffs. Equally, the globalisation of culture through products such as MacDonald's and Coca Cola should not be ignored. Hamburgers were new and exciting in the 1950s.

Activities

- Ask the children to look at the menus shown. They should then decide what country the food originated from, and make their own personal choices from the menus.
- Help the children to make the following international recipes:

Channa from the Caribbean

1. Soak 500g of chickpeas overnight.
2. Drain and dry in a cloth.
3. Heat cooking oil and deep fry the chickpeas until they are golden.
4. Put the chickpeas on a kitchen towel to absorb excess oil. Add salt and pepper.

Indian Coconut Squares

1. Mix 1 large can of condensed milk with 450g of icing sugar.
2. Stir in 300g of desiccated coconut until the mixture is stiff.
3. Add 4 drops of cochineal

WHERE HAVE YOU BEAN

to make the mixture pink.
4. Dust a tray with icing sugar. Press the mixture into the tray. When the mixture is firm cut it into squares.

- Ask the children to bring in food labels and display these around a map of the world, with arrows or pins and threads pointing to the country of origin.
- Use cookery books to discover more recipes from the original country of a migrant group that has affected British food culture, for example the Chinese, Italians or Indians. Make a display of these using illustrations from travel brochures or information packs from embassies.

Writing

- The former mill town of Bradford now promotes Asian culture as a tourist attraction, while Newcastle advertises its local China Town. Ask the children to design a take-away tour leaflet of your home area, with food from a different country every day. Include a route map, the name of the take-away and the type of food which is sold there.

Food today

A take-away meal in 1930 would probably have been fish and chips. Since 1945 people from other countries have come to live in Britain, and brought their local foods with them. Now we can choose from many exciting dishes.

● Look at these take-away menus and complete the table.
 Add your own favourites from take-aways near you.

Name of take-away	Country	My choice of food

 ● Design the cover for the menu of a new Indian restaurant or take-away called the Aagrah. Use library books about India or Indian food to help you with ideas.

© Folens (copiable page)

8 ways to help ...

There are many ideas in this book about developing and extending the photocopiable pages. Here are just eight ways to help you make the most of the **Ideas Bank** series.

1 Paste copies of the pages on to card and laminate them. The children could use water-based pens that can be wiped off, allowing the pages to be re-used.

2 Put the pages inside clear plastic wallets. They could be stored in binders for easy reference. The children's writing can again be easily wiped away.

3 If possible, save the pages for re-use. Develop a simple filing system so that the pages can be easily located for future use.

4 Use both sides of the paper. The children could write or draw on the back of the sheet, or you could photocopy another useful activity on the back.

5 Make the most of group work. Children working in small groups could use one page to discuss between them.

6 Photocopy the pages on to clear film to make overhead transparencies. The ideas can then be used time and time again.

7 Use the activity pages as ideas pages for yourself. Discuss issues and ideas with the class and ask the children to produce artwork and writing.

8 Customise the pages by adding your own activities. Supplement the ideas and apply them to your children's needs.